FOR THE CHANGING MOON

FOR THE CHANGING MOON

poems and songs

ANNA MARIE SEWELL

thistledown press

Thistledown Press Ltd.
410 2nd Avenue North
Saskatoon, Saskatchewan, S7K 2C3
www.thistledownpress.com

Library and Archives Canada Cataloguing in Publication
Sewell, Anna Marie, author
For the changing moon : poems and songs / Anna Marie Sewell.

ISBN 978-1-77187-168-6 (softcover)
I. Title.
PS8637.E932F67 2018   C811'.6   C2018-904565-5

Cover art: *Solstice 2012* by Trish Sewell
Author photo by Rebecca Lippiatt
Cover and book design by Jackie Forrie
Printed and bound in Canada

Canada

Thistledown Press gratefully acknowledges the financial assistance of the Canada Council for the Arts, the Saskatchewan Arts Board, and the Government of Canada for its publishing program.

I dedicate this book, with love to
Albina Hedwig/Albena Eileen (Sawchuk) Sewell (1933-2017),
who in her life lived with courage through many changes of the moon.

CONTENTS

MOON ON YOUR SHOULDER

THE OCCUPIED MOON

RIND OF WISHES MOON

MOON OF WOLVES

FORMULAE FOR MOON AND TIME

We begin with Thanksgiving. All good things do.

Welalin, Chi Megwetch, Hiy Hiy, Limlimpt
thanks, giving a soft chain across this land.

If we laid out the words, all the ways we say Thanks
would that song reach from here to the Moon?

MOON ON YOUR SHOULDER

CREATION SONG

They say, Star Woman fell
down here because
she was curious

they say, the star sisters
still watch us

they say, when star woman fell
it was a humble one
who gave all he had to reach
enough earth for her landing

they say, the humble ones
still watch us

they say, the turtle carries
on her shell sacred
geometries, formulae
for moon and time

they say, this is still
Turtle Island

they say, if you listen
the song goes on

sing, they say.

ONE MOON, MANY FACES

For Don, Rayanne, and the poets who walked the Autumn
Moon with me, September 2013. Also for Gerry, who knows
how to fit the moon into a teaspoon.

At the balance point between summer and autumn
so much turns on the breath of fog
falling over a broad green stream.

To be so pierced by light
vague, faceless sun
given specific, cratered glory.

And down in the water
is that you? Madam, your age is showing
and amplified, by each daughter
caught in hands, cups, rivers, ponds.

Each in our own night
we rise, turn, fill and give way.
Yes, yes.

But just now, no other moon
has ever risen just here, like this
silvering clouds, limning our path.

Put down your camera. Be quiet.
This is personal.

CHICKADEE: BEZHIG, READING

Imagine this, Anishinabemowin appears to Chickadee
turning the pages of a virtual dictionary
left online to reach back to the broken lines of human teachers.

In that same way, a poet opens a webpage and claws
words out, without knowing their grammar
flinging husks and snow and bits of dirt
hungry for their nourishment, afraid that she is not welcome
at the table where they feed; stupid proud and hungry angry
to wait for someone to tell her, *this how you say it, bird.*

apegish —	I wish that
akii-mazina'igan —	map
akina, akina gegoo —	everything
anishinaabewinikaade —	it has an Indian name
anokiiwinagad —	there is work
bashagiishkidibikad —	it is a dark night
bejibide —	it moves slowly
bekaa —	wait! slow down! hold on!
bezhig —	one
anang(oog) —	star
beshowad —	it is near, close by
biijibide —	it moves, it speeds, it lies here
biinad —	it is clean
biinde, biindig —	it is inside, inside
endogwen —	i don't know; i am not sure
eshkam —	gradually; more and more; less and less
eya' —	yes

ezhi —	thus; so; there
booch —	it is necessary; it is certain
gakijiwan —	there is a waterfall
ganabaj —	perhaps; maybe
ganawend -	takes care of it
gaa mashi —	not yet
gaagige- —	forever

ezhi   booch she will love these words.
Chickadee, find the will
to fight to the centre of the spill
of food, she will eat
grains from the ground and
grow round and . . .

FREE: FOR THE RAVEN'S SON

'You give too much,' he said, his arm
wrapped warm around my neck, almost
asleep, not quite lovers. Long since swallowed

our wavering footsteps side by side, even in
English, we barely spoke the same language but
he pulled my hand up against his heart
as we walked, and told me one more missing story
about one more brown girl gone.

A shaman would press through skin
into his brilliant heart pull out the shard
that vivisected him over and over.

Yes, she was too innocent, that girl. She was
a lot like me; but no. I did not tell
any missing stories of my own, to let us be
that much the same. The water too near, too deep.

So I let you hold my hand against your wild
raven's heart, took your story, walked you home.

But this is the price: never to be free of how
it feels to open your heart into someone's
hand and let them let you go.

OMIIMIIKAA — PLACE OF THE WILD DOVE
For Jorge, Black Coffee compañero

Omiimii — Passenger Pigeon.   Clear it away.
Massacre. Sacrifice. Last of her kind
in a zoo in Cincinnati, dying small
in a blaze of hot twentieth century
light, newsreel focused tight
on the theatre of war, in Europe, Whiteman's
Land, while here, no last stand, no grand plan
no destiny to hand on, branch to land on
this is the Jazz Age

but there was a time on this Turtle Island
when sky was shadowed from edge to edge
with wing beats, softly the dance of love.

Now the broken-hearted dreamers
in the Scientific tribe seek out
her DNA, smallest physical strand
with which to stitch her back
into the hand of life, erase erasure, bring her back home.

If you can do this — can you? Can you do this?
Can you bring back my father, too? Let him
spend his life singing, not gone
for a soldier the only way out. Can you
bring back my sister? So like a wild dove
without a place where she could land   *Omiimiikaa.*

Can you unclub the women tortured
by affluenzaed youth? Tell the truth
and reconcile those thousands more

fallen to the sociology of violent intervention
shadowing the sky *ai hai ai hai.*

They say the last twenty thousand
Omiimii refused to breed, had turned
their minds to silence, suicidal
empty in the heart, like the heartland
steel towns now.

Flint Michigan dying, Detroit rots
from the inside out
Oshawa and Windsor shudder
sleepless in their beds while
lights break one by one, shedding dark.

What is that whirring sound in the night?
Passenger pigeon ghosts in flight . . .

MAKING STEW

In the kitchen, Dad sat hunched like a bear in his corner
chair, cradled a battered grey metal teapot. *Three bag tea?*
Or just two? that's where I learned to make stew.

Old oak table, altar for holiday and mundane
butcher hogs, fish, chickens, steers, deer from the hunt
or moose. Cut it up full reverent, to which, don't draw
too much attention. *These are the things.*

That table could hold anything we threw at it. So
Dad and old Bert knew we would not suspect a trick
under tarp on the wagon in the yard, long black legs
waiting to be carried to the table.

Yeah, someone ran over Old Caesar. We gaped,
undone, gut-struck to tears. *Stop crying. Go look.* The punchline
hold steady, regardless of rumour and fear, believe it
when you see it. A horse hoof is not a moose hoof.

These are the things: tea, spilled pronouncements and
provocations,politics, philosophy, the great mystery of
proof, faith, how to sharpen a knife, the need
to honour lives given to ours. Everything happened
in the kitchen. And I learned to make stew.

KINDS OF MOON

There are so many: new full turning fading falling yammering
yellow dancer laughing deer moon
onion moon vegan moon, no fracking moon
the moon of marching activists, the occupied moon, the
moon of refusing to vote
disenfranchised moon shedding dark around your edges
black-handed moon, in the time of which,
you should beware my eyes and ward yourself

Sailor's moon, professorial moon of arena weddings

young moon, old moon, rind-of-wishes moon, teaspoon
moon, small and perfect; surfer moon, leaping wave to wave
yodeller's, moon of skin diseases, moulting moon;
never going back again
moon of remembering moon once hung by you

Moon of teen brothers, college girl moon, moon of wolves
and of taxicabs
O the moon when I've been up all night just walking
moon of river valleys, mountaineer's moon

The moon by which your eyes are endless
pinwheel portals to whole other galaxies, and
you so lazy lounged there by the pool

Moon of lozenges, homeopathic moon, moon for injections
supplementer's moon, empty moon of starch aisles glistening in
plastic wrap, and that wholistic moon enwreathed in kale

Moon of the wealthy, uptown moon, home-schooled
unbound homebrew moon, hiccuping down the sky, moon
of last chances

moon of fast glances, lap dances, bold gambles, boomerangs
to moon of reductive surgery, carved to fit the frame

Moon of your anger, corner moon, squeaking light on snow
you understanding what I was really trying to say, that moon
so thin and sharp it broke the sky open

Moon of volcanoes, moon of squid
moon of random parallels paradiddle
moon, drumrolling through the dark orchestral sky

Moon of capture, moon of if
the moon accidentally aligned
moon of weak arguments, moon of bald lies

Moon of diminishing returns, pocketbook moon
light folded in like so much Kleenex
the just in case moon

The moon on your shoulder
that one you carried, and the moon
trolling in your wake, moon of mud puddles
moon of glass, insipid little moon of tailored grass
moon I never answered, the bay gelding moon
fat sassy moon passed over, gone

Moon of renewable energy split, atomic
moon in crusts
of pallid glow on dragon
skins shed in limp swills
on dead sand
tsunami moon

we will begin again.

THE POEM OF SILENCE

. . . is for all those who never wrote . . .

. . . for what we all lost through the brutalities of the
Residential Schools (and Day Schools)
experiment . . .

. . . for the silences in the Canadian Canon of Literature
where there once was singing . . .

Margaret Atwood gave to Duncan Campbell Scott
eleven pages, for his poetry, she counted him worthy
of more pages than any other English language poet
in a supposed national anthology. Elegies to
the savage, no apology while overseeing murder, rape
starvation, medical experimentation, and that
contentious bone, whether to call it
genocide, cultural or otherwise.

. . . for all that, return to this page now, eleven times.

ATOMIC WORLD

On hearing an over-abstract jazz composition

This atomic world is nothing, broken
it is the happy fucking of atoms
that creates the orgiastic majesty.

Broken, this atomic world is random
strings of numbing nuance almost caught
together naked, but somehow ashamed.

Jazz, taken too far, lacks sex and flavour
(You say those words equivalate)
sound, music stripped to its atomic bones
by the same pretension that would say
that a car in parts strewn over the floor
could drive fast enough for a ticket, or at all.

This is idiot's babble, not even a baby's call for
breast and comfort, but the tragic thrash brain
uncoupled atomic, nothing but spastic
hand on blinded body without intent
melodic line, shape, form, meaning worship.

In the face of this monstrous pity renew the call:
All hail the molecular divine
conjugal marvel of life.
(You say, "Fuck, that was awful noise.")

SHE SANG

She sang *Coming Home* like her heart was
breaking, because she was
like a bird, poised to fly away
no stopping what she couldn't name.

We all walk wounded, all
afraid, she walked that way, but sang
as if she were brave, all the way from her cradle.
She sang in the basement, the one private space
Pat Benatar and Barbra Streisand
through the vents, a concert in rubbled concrete.

She was my sister, afraid
of the dark, but more afraid there'd be no way
out of a small place that did not want
smart and pretty, and talented and mixed
not fitting White nor Native mold, no holding
her down. She sang herself brave.

She sang through her jazz school juries
for judges, not saying her fiancé lay
in an early grave, fallen undeclared
they were waiting 'til school was done.
Too emotional, they told her. Broken, she sang.

My sister sang in Carnegie Hall, a farmgirl
halfbreed, singlehandedly talked producers into
adding five Indigenous women to the bill of an
international choral festival, no other group less
than sixty strong; her group, along for the ride;
fame they still use, though they refused

to sing her songs, because she was too pushy, when
another tour brought them to her homeland.

Wounds all round, plenty of wounds to go around.

Once she was gone, some woman
told my child she could tell her all about
her aunty, my sister, as if I were not standing there
or as if that woman had sat with her when she
composed and arranged her funeral song.

These stories open out into layers of wounds
and reasons, rights and wrongs, the flawed
diamonds of community and relationships
different from every side. Or else they fly
away, like every life does in the end.

Boil it down to what matters.

As for her, she sang.

LIGHT ON THE WINGS

O, the holiness of red ash berries
chickadees stumbling drunk from branches.

I will spare a paean of praise
for seasoning of cold
darkness teeming with seeds

where raw-cheeked prayer comes tumbling
kicked breathless into startled dance
walking on black ice.

O, the holiness of dove grey wings
Whiskeyjack snickering from feeder to feeder.

Once, in walking twilight up from
Hawrelak Park, falling behind
my companions, I saw through gathering dark

an image of us walking
darker mountains, sharper trail
longer journey, long ago.

O, does the ghost of our days refract? in frostlight
forward, glance off winter wings on into unknown lives.

HUNTING SEASON

I've felt your sharp glance cut my way
throwing leaves of gold, dry promises
when sun's gone south of the river the hunter comes, you
glide by my door, northwestering
stalking the season's edge.

Listen: I can't outrace you can't
outpace you. Not without grace, frost
morning's breath with your warning:
my home is yours when you will.

Do you see me shiver? Is that why
you whisper purple leaves of willow
grace my sidewalks with cape of lace
cast down so I may walk in song
the while the leaves are chanting

can't outrace you can't outpace

Hunter, you whisper, time has come
now lay the fire and set the feast
the drink is warm, your home is mine

I have been warned, so lead my dance
enchant me with a fox trail draped
down Mill Creek's shoulder all ablaze
with pembina, you vow to write
a love song, chickadees upon my open hand
your need like rowans lit by wilder rhythms
beads of blood against darkened sky.

THE OCCUPIED MOON

SHAPE SHIFTING

Real Indians, the shape-shifting kind, they're gone
now, if they ever were more than fantasy.That's tragedy,those
owers lost to us, look at us now. We're not those, people can't
do that, only got stories. Well, I've told a few myself, from time
to time, and here's one now: my father was a shape-shifter.
How? Constitutional entrenchment of Métis as a People.

That might not count. You don't think so? Maybe you wanted
to hear it like late at night, all shivering round the table
some smoky old story about those ones who turned into dogs
or bears, or flying beings. No, I never saw him walk as a bear
or a dog, or in feathers and wings, but I saw him on TV.

Disenfranchised Anishinaabe, orphaned Mi'gmaq, church
school survivor went working in the bush, broke a leg and
turned into a guitarist. Singer, trainer, teacher, army sergeant
farmer, trucker, taught himself house mover's physics
and Robert's Rules of Order.

On TV, we spied him by his hat, that one he always wore for
meetings, ironically, a cowboy hat. Dad at the tables
in Ottawa in 1982, committee committed, Métis Delegation
shifting the shape of our nation.

CHICKADEE: BOOCH, SURVIVING

maamawi — all together
gabe-dibik and gabe-giizhik — all night and all day

songs she never learned
leak down the rocks

geyaabi	still
dabinoo'igan(an) —	shelter(s)
dawaa —	there is space; there is room
dewe'igan(ag) —	drum(s)
dibaajimowin —	story; narration of events
endaayang —	our (inclusive) house
endaayaan —	my house
endaso —	so many
endaso-dibik —	every night
endaso-giizhik —	every day
giinawaa —	you (plural)
giinawind —	we, us (inclusive); you and i
giinetawind —	we, us (inclusive) alone; we, us
only	

(well, anyhow) it starts to grow

maajiishkaa —	it starts moving
maamakaadendaagwad —	it is astonishing
maamakaaj —	amazing!; strange!
maamawi —	all together

when the storm hits, birds huddle together to survive; unless
they have to fly, in which case, each needs wing room, lest they
break like waves one on the other.

RAEANN ♫
Blues rock in E for JME.

The look in your eyes tells me all i need to know
he's got you walking that road again
you were so proud of it, but things have changed a bit
for you, RaeAnn

You were the one who could make us laugh, RaeAnn
saw the song in the simplest things
but you listened to the wind and heard the wings
wings of eagles, wings of owls, someone coming
to carry you to a place where you can't stand

And RaeAnn, don't you wanna go home?
Hey RaeAnn, don't you wanna go home?

That was the year you lost your family
say dying it's just a northern thing
well, dying is easy, living is hard
when the days are long and the nights so dark
can't you seem to see the spark, RaeAnn?

And RaeAnn, don't you wanna go home?
Hey RaeAnn, don't you wanna go home?

[1]I saw the Northern Lights
blaze a dance across midnight skies
I saw your hand reaching out
I saw your hand reaching high

---

1   *drop down to Dm, Am, Em, slow it down for the bridge*

A look in your eyes tells me all i need to know
he's got you walking that road again
you couldn't make it stick, now you're stuck with it
ain't the needle such a perfect fit, RaeAnn?

And RaeAnn, don't you wanna go home?
Hey RaeAnn, don't you wanna go home?

The Black Donnellys, ice cold water down the back of you
— activist, openly mixed race, worst of all, poor, barefaced
and smart — otherwise, you forget what night might hold.

Harlequin Romances, fifty cents apiece or traded amongst
ladies who'd long since cut their bargain with the Lord and
society; literate and free, inside the mind, where love blooms
(if one is pert, and takes care to have heart-shaped face, tip-
tilted nose, cupid's-bow mouth.)

Halfbreed, by Maria Campbell, the only extant Native Lit
on offer from your high school English teacher, never mind
you had no clue what the narrator meant by 'on the streets'
nor so many euphemistic passages presaging life-paths to be
waved in your face presuming you must choose from
these tropes, and these alone.

Watership Down, which you glared upon dubiously
this atonement from grade seven Spelling teacher
after your parents read her the Riot Act: no more docking
marks for doodling on perfect tests done rabbit fast.

What has a rabbit to do with ships of any kind? you
suspected World War II, now ever after
'down the rabbit hole' means only one place for you
and all those intrepid companions.

(Totems and guides, totems and guides, pages of them).

YOGA: LETTING GO THE MOON

I swear beneath the moon
for letting go
I have loved you, and I love you still
all that you were, so much of which I never saw
all that you might have been, which was hidden
perhaps from you
all the roads you suffered down
and all the times you rose

For letting go
I have hated you, at times, that's true
all that you held back and refused to share with me, all
that you railed against, selfishly, never admitting all that
you would have given me, had I known how to
love you more truly, all that the world has
missed out on, not just me, although it is
personal, this great love, this great hatred.

Look around, beloved, the world is fat
with holding
on to all we crave, with grasping
after this one thing: to be loved, to be
absolved of dancing
absolutely carved into the hand of life
that hand wide open.

How to let this go? How?

MELTWATER

On the train thru the rockies

this land is old in human terms
before labels and explorers
posit one man (though there were many)
whose language sang of this
rocky way, and meltwater in the spring

try to imagine him imagining this, railway
and the passage; well, you can't

conjure word, sound, cadence his imagined reaction

and this is your lump of coal-black grief
that fuels your train of thought when you
shunt quick and loud away
hissing steam, young country
immigrants, wilderness, all one track

there is no gauge for beyond, you cannot talk to him
(nor his imagined relatives) therefore
you burn in proximity to his descendants
stutter out rhythm, cry over meltwater
something you have no words for

DOWN BY THE MARY BURLIE

Down by Mary Burlie park, stands a tree
who shades the way up to steel roofed
pavilion where the homeless rest —

The Homeless, that tribe we are all
so close to, one step away if you believe
boot strappers, anyone could fall in there
as if there are no marks of rank, no
subtle indicators.

It might be more like a guild, memberships
due to generations of struggle, a seed
of abuse and neglect, and unhealed
anger that drives senseless reactionary living
existing, getting by, not getting past it.

On top of the Mary Burlie parkland stands
a monument not to these people, but some
others fallen far away, forgive me
bootstraps aside, they never walked here
nor pleaded, as they plead now in bronze for
their imagined lives, not the unwashed
unloved rabble gathered hand to mouth
beneath a grain bin roof, a two-fisted view:

on one hand, a statue of all they need to be
for their fall were to be counted; on the
other, a tree full of sparrows.

TICKET TO RIDE

My dad rode a camel. So what?
So do millions of tourists. So

Church school survivor, bush Indian
disenfranchised by his father's death
left school, went to the logging camp run
by his uncles, his Elders who handed him
work, a man's measure.

Non-Status, unsubstantiated, Dad
voted while still-Status family could not
though they, too, were welcome
to take up arms for 'our' country.

See Dad on a camel, and behind him
in horizon's haze there is a twelve year old
boy with his dog, walking into winter
cold, away from his own private wars.

Pride is a ticket to ride as far as your own
eyes, heart and gut can make it.

MOON LUNE LUNA PERSONAL
  For La Belle Giselle

En el fulcro   au point d''quilibre balance
point between *l'été y otoño*
la niebla lleva tanto   sur le souffle
de la brume breath of fog *cayendo* falling
tombant sobre un flujo   river
fleuve broad and green   *verde y ancho.*

¿Como es posible? vivir así traspasado
D'être ainsi transpercé par la lumière so pierced by light
por la luz del sol anónimo su vaguedad flou vague
faceless sun   *doué d'une gloire spécifique, cratérisée*
clarificada, cratered   *gloire* glory *gloria.*

Y por debajo del agua ¿podría ser?   vers le bas sous
l'eau down in the water *est-que c'est vous?*
Madame, Madam, *Señora se anota su vejez   votre âge*
parait your age *amplificada et amplifié* amplified *en cada*
hija each daughter *chaque fille attrapée*
caught in hands, cups, rivers, ponds *en manos vasos, ríos*
charcas dans les mains, des tasses, des rivières, des étangs.

Each in our own night *nuit por derecho proprio*
chacun de nous nous élevons we rise, turn, fill and give
way *nos alzamos, cambiamos, nos llenamos nous*
nous remplissons et cédons de luz solo por devolver
claro, que sí clairement, oui yes yes.

But just now *en ce moment,*
aucune autre lune, no other moon, *ninguna otra luna*
a déjà levé juste là, juste comme ça risen just here, like this
exactamente aquí, asi
plateando los nubes, dando lirismo al sendero. baignant les nuages
d'argent, silvering clouds, limning our path, *lyrisme du chemin*
se ha levantado.

Deja la cámara. Deposez votre caméra. Put down
your camera, be quiet. *Quedate callado, restez*
tranquille. Ceci est personal. Es personal
personal.

ABECEDARIO ANIMAL

Aardvarks of Apprehension sniff your soul's toes; Bees of
Defensiveness fizz in your ear; is that
the Crocodile of Doubt?

Dung Beetles of Exactitude roll on, while
the Ermine of Excuses slinks through; Temporality's
Ferrets stop digging for nothing; but Love
is that hulking Gorilla, watching from the shadows; he
grooms himself and eats a casual leaf, undeniably.

Horses of Hyperbole stretch out their silly
necks and run, swifter than the sun;
and o, the Iguanas of Infamy . . .

Jealousy's Jackass kicks hard;
Kingfishers of Kindness stitch up my heart
in gentle arabesques. Now
let Lions of Laziness loll lascivious, lest
the meddlesome Mink of Memory shimmy in
to remind me, moving
heaven and earth.

Newts of Curiosity wake me in the dawning; onward
Ostriches of Realistic Expectation run
and kick your mighty legs!

Perhaps, perhaps, perhaps those are
the Porpoises of Rapprochement bobbing
in ebbing wavetops, reading the news.

Reputations Quetzals may flash long green tails, but
Craft in the path is a simple brown Quail.

Run, Rabbit of Regret, or risk
my wrathful rap, rapscallion.

Consider Serenity's Scorpion, basking
well-defended in indiscriminate sun.
Ah, Tarantula of Tenderness, lurking
in the tight-bunched Bananas of Righteous
Indignation, ready to creep up my arm.

Uakari of Unexpected Beauties, light my path
with your clear and present gaze.
haHA! Those are the Vicuñas of Victory, their pointy toes
tap-dancing all over any protest against persistent gloriousness.

Now let fuzzy little Wombats of Self-regard protect me
from the host of provocations to be less than.

There go the X-ray Tetras of Independence. How
do they school their thoughts, discern the flow, inhabit it so
fluently?

Yaks of Self-possession, we go
to tea, all woolly and reeking of Life.

O, holy Zebu of Right Relationship, lift up
my heart on horns of thankfulness, for all
that is, and my place in this.

(But of course, i never forget the Moose of Inspiration, blowing
his mighty nose in the ear of my mind. They say the Moose
has a thing going on with the Elephant of Surprise, they're
so often seen together.)

TURTLE ISLAND EASTER PRAYER

O Lord, renew me, body, heart, mind, this soul

O you Good Spirits, you Saints who intercede:
budge aside, if you don't mind just enough to let me
speak to Manidoog i do not know, whose names
and specialities were not passed down.

Holy Mother, some of your children stand in my way;
be kind and thank them for the good they do, then bid
them take a seat, so Manidoog i did not meet
may step lightly forward, lightly shining.

Tell me, shall we forgive each other?
Yous, for stepping back when these pushier gods
came caterwauling; me, for not knowing Your names
that i might intercede on your behalf, co-creation being
the law, and show that you are as loved and wanted
as needed as ever.

Great Mother say You love us all; Heavenly Father
that is the word, by which, only say it, i am healed.

At a crossroads, Yous and i, ever so; today, let me
choose a good road. Let me walk in the shine of all
Your loves reconciled. Down here i have work to do.

WAITING FOR GENHIS KHAN

Smoke in the air? I drove here through haze
like a desert sandstorm. Doesn't bother me.
Don't smoke, she said, *it lowers your count.*

Stupid people everywhere get to breed like flies, me
I get the nag, like it's my fault we live in this
cancer-water hole, 'til some Towelhead rigs the price
back down. But she likes the money. While it's rolling
I should let her hang me out to dry?

Where is my horse and my banner?
You're not fit to drive, she said. I am not unfit
to ride, and I read all the Mongols were raging
alcoholics, drunk the whole time they rampaged.
They sure weren't mincing up tofu and lettuce
like soup could make a man of anyone.

I got here. I paid for this. I'll drink 'til when the Khan
and his armies rise again, and ride down 63
looking for takers, then I'm signing on.
If Genghis were here now, you'd not manhandle me.
I'm being cut off?! I'd cut you off! We'd bust this place
open, and your wenches would open their thighs, serve me
in all ways, damn your eyes, I will smoke!
Do you not smell the reek of his imminent ride?

*You could get a degree, she said. You're not stupid. Why
do you act so —* Well why would I waste tens of thousands for
license to raise one pinkie in the air? I am
what I am, a man drinking to

39

the Resurrection, the Insurrection, the Intersection
of myth and history and this godforsaken century
needs a king, a Khan, I'm signing on

when he gets here. 'Til then, another round
and another. To Hell with your rules, I am
a Beast, waiting for a Beast, waiting for the signal.
All this smoke, it's his spirit calling, clear the way.

My Khan and I, we will ride. Burn the world.
Burn it all clean.

RIND OF WISHES MOON

DARK SEASON PRAYER

If he rode in this moment
rolled in and roared
Burn it all down!
You would. We would

hitch our bloody names to his standard
ride out
like Revolution, a Golden Horde
like every fire ever lit, burn wild
right through the matted tangle of all this.

Hit me now
with the Sky God's hammer
break me free, I itch
inside this woolly shell

Unleash the hell, the holiness of fire
the rage, the rage of unshackled North.

SELF HATRED

in a moon of summer
so much taken from us

car accident, but he had a vision first
and had been beaten at every turn

so he turned to the path of last resistance
whiskey, pills, rage, cigarettes
he ate the words of bullies
and spat out his own demise.

cancer, but she refused western medicine
ashamed of the extortionate cost, and her family
without that kind of money, and her experience
of the rest of the world, anyone moneyed that way
would only make her feel small
should she admit she could not afford
pills to counteract the side-effects

so much for hope
and the body's strength.

these words don't talk back
they want only to reconnect
the broken lines
like moon on a surface shattered
still, for those of you

who also
shiver at the touch of memories

all we lose when we cannot bind
the wounds we did not give, but could not take.

PRICING

> *"You Were Poor, and You Went to School Knowing You Were Poor"* — Anna Maria Tramonti, to Eric Gerard, regarding his crisis in law school.

You went to school knowing you were poor.

You were poor and you went to town knowing you were poor.

At dances you held up the wall, though
noone would name it, bride price flashed
around and past and the band played on.

"If her daddy's rich, take her out for a meal
If her daddy's poor, just do what you feel"
— "In the Summertime", American pop song

Poor, learn to budget what you actually need
food, shelter, clothes that match asskicking
shoes, to sound out bone strong arrogance.

Write your own songs, your own ticket, sit
where you want, stand alone, hold out for
someone who can dance for real, for free.

UNRECONCILED

To any of us who has ever
just quietly raged alone
because we simply want
to be heard without weeping
to be known without bleeding
to be loved when we win:

I pledge to you
that i will not require of you
that you break, in order
to love you, for being
evidence of life in spite of it all.

Thank you for being
simply for being.

ASHES IN THE MAKING
After Agha Shahid Ali's Even the Rain

You seem to dance like morning's leaves in brightest hue
a grove of secrets burning, ashes in the making.

No lover ever naturally delighted in the view
of his or her heart's desire as ashes in the making.

Black shoals of coal wrenched from their river beds to fuel
power stations feeding light, shed deadly ashes in the making.

Those poets who freely scattered seeds, they knew
the most dazzling hope has bitterest ashes in the making.

She never shared her bed with any one addicted to the blue
consuming smoke, yet she found ashes, in the making.

The alchemy of bread by which the fallen grain renews
leaves ghosts of water, beds of ashes in the making.

Watch ghostly elders wisp and totter down railings to the pool
lighter than water now, they float like ashes in the making.

Now clothe your heart quiescent to season's turning, Sewell
green leaves make autumn's fire, for ashes in the making.

SAY THAT HE SHALL BE GIVEN TO THE KING OF THE SEA
For Tooker Gomberg, and for Gilbert Bouchard

he has gone into the water mouth open singing
it cannot be that he meant this song, yet he is gone

if the rag and bone of him be recovered, still he is
gone, green light extinguishing light

he has married his heart to the ceaseless
rush gone into the water

say that he shall be given to the king of the sea
whose palace had a space for him

say that in his descending
green fish and gilled maidens took his arms
shush shush susurrating softly slipped him through
weed and rock, tumbled in mud, decorated with
all those fallen breaths uncounted

say he went accompanied to rest and feast and tell tales
to the king of the sea, who had awaited bright witness
who cradled him to his craggy breast and cried
softly, *my son my son*
you are too soon
but well
come, my son.

SAY THAT WRONG MEDICATION KILLED HIM
For TG and GB, too, and all those left to mourn

warp in the medicine
bitter taste of trust

he swallowed down
to blunt and soften mind
calm the heart

into the glide
where green gilled maidens
fish, the little people
wait, border watchers
rocking, down
the pill led him

down, he shed his
too speedy heartbeat
in favour of surrender
into sea time
washing away

then all that is left
is to wonder if
he brought his soul
as an offering, softest gold
to appease the king of the sea

or whether he rocks there now
another soul down, under water
leveller
impending
rising tides

START MAKING SENSE
After David Byrne, long after.

We are not chaos.
We are not powerless.
We are not shadowless.
Not too small.

This one's for generations lost
swallowed like their drugs
into the sleep that brings no vision
into the cold cold river and gone

into the belly of the beast
amnesia.

Listen, listen well.

If it were right, I'd throw a net
of poetry you could not slip through
bind you here when you would slide
out by the eye of a needle
like biblical camels

borrowed mythological
beasts of amnesia.

We are not shadowless
not too small, not nothing at all
it is not just days going by.

It's not too late to feed the dreams
who tread this land beneath the scream
of songs that have no shadows.

Would they spring up now
if honestly, we call them?
The Water Cats, Banaabekwe
Thunderbird and the Little People
rocking in their shadows, riding this
one out, sitting out this dance of madness
would they return to pierce the belly
of this beast?

We are not chaos. We are
beholden to our dreams, to gather up
our sticks and slips of consequence
and set our signal light, and in this coming night
start making sense.

Remember this, the teeth of mountains
rising in our sights, remember grass and open hands
and dancing, through the aspen arboured days

Remember when the starfields
show their cold white face etched high above
they turn in sequence, unrelenting
making sense.

We are so small, but not nothing at all.
We are not shadowless, nor powerless
nor chaos, nor alone.

The belly of the beast amnesia never will be filled
so feed it, instead, to the real dreams, let it
feed the beast of reckoning, feed the beast of
yes, the beast of history named, set free to wreak
the dance of tell, and hear, accept, confess

this is no empty land, and underground
the water flows with names, with names.

In simple ceremonials to bind us into light
we build our bed inside this night and rest
with love as our defence

and tied once more between the shadows
of what was and what can be, then let the past
forgive the future, let every beast regain their name
put down your timid art's pretence

start making sense.

PATHS AND HILLS
For Tony, and the good people of Ayabe, ghosts and all

had we known, we might have never
sweat stung by whip thick spider webs
flung at face level, cut by knife-edged
leaves, scratched up that hillside, in thrall

no path, but something wreathed green, to discover
silence when we asked people.

barely beginning to be written, driven by histories
nonetheless, if not the ones we found there
no names, no faces, smooth stones

in dappled green, the infant dead in hilltop nursery
enshrined. dangling threads, heads bent we toppled
down the path laid on the quiet side, big bamboo
clacking, checked our shoulders, easy to hold onto.

across the valley, i had climbed the first hill alone

red, well-trodden road through pine and cedar, water
springing, tin ladle laid by, obasans chirring like
cicadas, breezing by. take your time, they smiled.

at the peak, a view, the valley fat with rooftops
one particular green hill, and here, unlikely bright
fifteen foot tall tuning fork, tiny hammer dangling.
you strike it, so, to ring out peace.

peace? for the world, if you want, they smiled.
what they kept from me, what they knew.

WOOD SUITE

1. The Will

What looks like boldness: break down instruments and use parts to rebuild other broken down instruments. But Dad was practiced at métissage; six children's worth of testimony to one human race.

Besides which, there's Will. Not in some post-sixties, hippy-trendy, read-it-in-a-Carlos-Castaneda-book kind of way, yet when first Castaneda book jumped off a used bookstore shelf I took it as a 'howdy' from beyond.

Howdy, and look sharp: how much Don Juan withheld, how much he played upon the tropes given, and the hunger for real true magic.

There isn't any, incidentally.

2. The Way

What passes for boldness: sudden move after long examination, song sprung instantly from bed where it germinated,
long scarifying winter hunt for lines that codify
and confirm, take pains, you can see through mountains.

And that's not magic, either.

3. The Memory of Wood

My friend Stephen spoke of envisioning wood singing
around him one night in an old house, and so it is: wood
breathes even after death, can bend, rebound, resonate
resound, never ceases to harbour song.

And you can make of that what you will.

4. Unreasonable Colour

I dropped my one guitar on concrete, broke his neck. Guitar
shop pro said let it go, but my friend Eric lent studio space
growled around intervening, gruff-voiced, eyes on wood with
suspicious brightness as it began again to gleam.

Old-time expert mourned when he heard we'd come to the
point of applying new finish, said I'd surely killed its voice. He
didn't add that it was worse because I was a woman, my
hands suspect on craftsman tools;

and it is true, i stained it emerald blue.

5. Root Chord

Mutt thing, this and that piece nailed and glued and coaxed
together in yellow light, farmhouse kitchen far beyond reach
of teachers, one displaced Indian lays upon the oaken table
one more body, this one of wood, not to cut and package
for the freezer, but to bend, sculpt, manage by eye and ear and
unschooled hand, with hammer and knife, smoke and will
until it is made.

In telling you I took this guitar with me when I travelled the
world, I have already said too much. Now you know what
I am, bits and pieces put together out of ancestral dreams, no
specialist knowledge, no specialist tools. Such places as it fits
together, it is held by any sort of glue, nail, bolt or random
plastic. That is the nature of this made creature:
unreasonable.

> No secret. No magic.
> No long apprenticeship, except
> the one owed to The Song.
> The root of it all is knowing
> wood will hold song.

CHICKADEE: MINO, MAAZHI

A hungry bird will land wherever food is found.

mandaamin —	corn; kernel of corn
mandaaminaaboo —	corn soup
manoomin —	wild rice; rice
mandaaminaak(oon) —	(ear of) corn

eye of newt, tongue of battered
stands of continuance

memwech —	just that; it is so
mii sa —	and so
mii'iw —	that's it
mindookad —	there is dew
mino —	good
minogin —	it grows well
mangademo(n) —	the trail or road is wide
megwayaak —	in the woods
megwe —	
megwekob —	in the bush
miskwaanakwad —	the clouds are red

you know, like in an evening sky
the fire blazes up   like

miskwi —	blood
mitagoonag —	on the snow
mitashkosiw —	on the grass
mitakamig —	on the ground
miziwe —	all over; everywhere

miziwebii'igaade —
miziweshkaa —
maazhi —

easy for you to flit from place to place, picking
this or that thing you like, as if taste is your only
obligation.

miziweyaa —   it is whole
naawayi'ii —   in the midst of it

right smack dab in the middle

nagamon(an) —   song, songs
nagamowin(an) —   song, songs

singing

nandawendaagwad —   it is suitable, desirable

naniizaanad —   it is dangerous

nashke —   behold!

look out, those people out there dancing, what they're doing is
evil
is illegal, is pagan and savage and fruit of the devil and if you go
you will never come back, you will never

niimi'idi —   they dance
niimi'idiwin —   dance

what is more intransitive
intransigent
insolent

maazhi —

is that the thing you fear there, out in the woods there? a
gathering
where you cannot go, unless you swear to protect what's there

niinawind —   we, us (exclusive)
nindoodem(ag) —   my totem, clan

MOON OF WOLVES

GO HOME MOON
"go home moon, the party is over" — *Mr. Yegpie*

this is the moon who wants
to sleep on my sofa, cry
on my shoulder, hold on
to the worst of her secrets

she tells me only that which
she judges I will bear
without leaping up
raging with fists to the sky

did you see her
silver shoulders rise
above the careless
conversation? see
her mark the exits
note the time, reach
for the bottle

now she's got her glow on
now she'll be okay

sea of tranquility
pale grey face

sea of tranquility
limited grace
see her spin

through the clouds
of careless conversation
see her light
on the corners, the edges
of things, she is waiting

i have built a room
safe for the moon
to come home to
it has to be enough

MITTENS
For Daniel Patrick Cole, full of grace.

Smitten
with pride guilt old memories
we know what it is to be
seen and not heard.

Without pride
guilty always guilty of being
wrong
place face ability
not strong
not heard.

We knit together something
thumb by thumb
gesture by gesture.

Bring me the baddest boy in the room!
Look at us, we are the same.

How could it be? that
nobody wanted you
to succeed.
How could it be? that nobody
reached out
toward the spark
warmth in you.

Here now
take this
take my hand
warm your own.

Let this cover all the things
we won't say, in language that nests
rustling between us, and lets
drop feathers
all through our days
from now on.

Let this cover handshakes
let this cover comfort
let this stand
for what we are
a pair
brought together to make
the world warmer.

KNIT

To our Elders, with respect, especially Betty Loree.

What is this hole? She wonders fretting
her grey cardigan with knotted fingers.

She will not ask aloud, she decides
in case he says, it is the same one that you left
my baby toes to poke through in the cold.

She will not ask in case he remembers
red-faced, bawling feebleness crying, crying
her young self too slow to respond.

What is this break? She wears
time's lines like a map for trains
clack of knitting needle years.

Did she string the loom of his life too loosely
fail to hold the line? When his chubby fists
hammered fledgling rhythms on her skin, she said
he lacked the words to make known his needs, but
did he know, when she did not, that she was faking
serenity to let him flail, while she seethed

inside, caught up in the act of will that kept her
from raising her hand to him, when she so
easily, so vividly could see him roll and break
shocked silent once without thought.

Is it that thought now upon her own cheek?

She rocks. She plucks threads. Shadows gather, night
will fall, like accusations, whispering its condemnations
conjuring too many could-have-beens. Her weary head.

What thread would it take to bind this? Unravel
knots between when we come into this world sacred
and sacred take our leave.

What is this light? She wonders, gazing at her
son, the life long dream imperfect beams.

And he rests her cheek upon his shoulder, wraps
her in new wool the colour of wild roses, gift of
comfort, after all, within reach, however uncertain
the knit, however holey, wholly holy.

THE MORTAL SUMMER
Edmonton, 1989

I left before the leaves could fall
flew south with my guitar
green Hudson Bay blanket
disc camera, tape deck, notebook

long seasonless year in blue skies
bougainvillea, Chapala with her *lirios*.

Chapala under mountain shoulders
carreterra lined with horses, dead grim
greening punctuation, walk to town singing.

This secret path, breathed chubby Juan
that rock, *Maestra*, where they change Man
to Jaguar; they can read red markings.

We are in large part composed of slanting
sun.

Up here, where we Round Dance, sun
swings wide in his yearly parade, each
summer's green-limned days long beyond
probable, for such a short time

Shed Catholicism, run naked on a dare
lope into red twilight streets
alive alive alive.

EDMONTON IN WINTER: THIS PEHONÂN

1. Outside

country people don't throw snow
in your face they know the distance between
you and fire might prove fatal

it is only when the fire is close and proven
that we dare to laugh and douse our skin

2. Inside

this pehonân, and we, savages who fled
south following sun's arc, nomad economies
dictating shape of a do-able size

no cities here before oil, call that proof of
lack of civilization, but these days beckoning
sun can't even clear thirty-year-old trees, and
economies of wealth mean
only the wealthy can follow the sun

3. In the Dark

missionary stories tell of leaving
the old, the halt, the lame to die out in
ice, the snow, clean hard wind

now, cloaked in houses
burning the future, we tough it out
wait for the sun to return.

BUSH-WHACKING
Edmonton 2009

north bank
north saskatchewan
late in the year
early rimes of ice too sharp and shallow
force us up the bank as ankle-busting trees
hunch knees above highwater line

we threaded trails of small things
tramped through literature of their lives

the children pipe and flutter
unconsciously magpie
through ruined clinker brick
foundations of things once steady
somebody's hearth and home
and look, a work-sized horse shoe

my friend knew things about ropes
showed me how to hold the line between us

the children shriek and whimper, depending on
our judgment, cling to stout cord, hand over
hand across a concrete cleft obstructing
our path, providing outflow for the city
unaware above the bank of what passes
below, scribbling in the understory

we were sound in certainty
once this trail was known.

THINGS YOU GIVE UP

arranging six
small cups on
your kitchen
window sill
so that the plum
blossom
design arcs
from cup to cup around
a perfect curvature

wondering
whether the world
has a place for you
that curvature is now
perfected

BARRA DE NAVIDAD, THE NEW YEAR'S EVE

My sister was scared to leave our room.
Anything could happen out there, she said.
So we played cards in the fug of cheap hotel
until boys with guitars passed in the hall
and I threw in my hand and deserted her.

Anything could happen out there, I said.
Cards on the table, I was thinking
of me, not of her fiancé who fell
from a balcony, nor of the hard dark
northern years before that, her
first-to-leave courage, anger over
fear. I was fighting for my own light
all in, whether or not she would follow.

When the New Year's stars stooped
down over Navidad Bay
she was the one who danced
with handsome Fernando, just met.

I was the one writing in sand, with one finger
Megwetch, Megwetch, Megwetch.

LAKESONG ♫

Play in any key, using basic folk 1-4-5 chord progression,
midtempo, sloping along. Flourish and embellish as you like.

I have outlasted the cynical, who've outlasted their fear
And seen the tough boys open up and shed their honest tears
And then gone and embarrassed them by speaking of their heart
With no excuse except that it's (demanded by) my art.

And if you think I'm walking brave by making these things
known
Then let me set you straight, I am a coward to the bone
I've let the decades glide like Indians, like old Paul Simon said
And spent too many years locked in my head.

I have faced eternity while drowning in a lake
And prayed the Lord most pitifully not my soul to take
With nothing more to offer but my poems and my mistakes
I asked if he had any mercy spare I'd like some if he'd give
I simply had to say, I want to live.

You'd think if I was bargaining that I would have a chip
But I never could lie to the Lord, I never was that hip
I said you've seen my blundering for thirty years by now
I don't see I'll be changing much somehow.

And if you let me live, I'll likely go on as I am
A mildly clever poet and an unabashed ham
And if you let me live, I'll keep on following this song
The one I have been following so faintly for so long
And I won't say I'll get much clearer, but I'll sing.

I won't find the cure for cancer, and I won't end the war
And I won't heal out history, nor uplift all the poor
I 'll just keep on writing poems, much as before.

Good enough, said the Lord, and his hand carried me along
So I have got to reason there's a reason for my song
When other souls more worthy have been taken home too fast
The grace of god is all that lets us last.

So now you know the story of why I can't live in doubt
An unfit swimmer overmatched and arrogant set out
Ran out of air and power had to lie upon my back
And tell the truth to God and sky and finally just ask
To live, just as I am, not perfect, bold or brave
Not overly exceptional, no paragon of might
Just me, and I'm alive and it's alright.

LONELY PLANET

Lonely planet, do you have to roll? ceaselessly
onward uncaring as a wave, singlehandedly
clearing the seaboard, so much for our nuclear dreams.

Why, we wondered, do they say it's the tongue
that gets tied? sitting on your hand-built table, hearts
stuttering, like the bubbling spring nearby.

Hesitating, there always seemed another
weekend, in which I might search out the path
above the city, walk Daimonji, tracing fire.

There are three songs that call you home:
geese, chanting, with their wing-feather drone
thread of swans in unprovoked threnody
this drum in my ear, fading, returning.

One folding tatami that never came in the mail
carries the city of Kyoto, those hills beyond
the seasons, sun, rain and wind folded away for
memories, now untraceable.

THE DRUNKEN BICYCLES
For Harriet and Stephanie

Off Kiamachi
green Zen flag weeds
festoon bent wheels

And there, below High Level Bridge
shopping carts slow migratory chevrons

In every heart a notch where first rays
light in every single heart

O rogue shopping carts, O drunken
bicycle veering, random shear
lunging down to ravage water

Maybe we should all get drunk and kiss
softly, with gentle consensual intent
whenever we see dark clouds overhead

Sacrifice more shopping carts to Kisiskâtchewanisîpi
so fast-flowing river who binds city to banks, will let
the sad and desperate pass, find beds more warm

Loving tonight, like drunken bikes off Kiamachi
bridges satisfy Kamogawa's hunger, ward off
hara-kiri see melancholic latter-day samurai
home.

THEY PLAY MAPLE SUGAR ♫

*Play with the chord changes of Ward Allen's mighty "Maple
Sugar", to which and whom this is a tribute, and let the words
and melody play around that as they will for you.*

They play "Maple Sugar"
And it carries me back home
Dancing in the kitchen
With my crazy Uncle John
And with those Northern Lights all shining
For the loved ones dead and gone
We sing the song within our hearts to carry on

We grew up with the wood stove
and the outhouse and the dark
with the soft breath of the West Wind
with the East Wind's hard remarks
with the push to keep your distance
with the push to stand your ground
with the songs that spun the dancers round and round

They play "Maple Sugar"
And it carries me back home
Dancing in the kitchen
With my crazy Uncle John
And with those Northern Lights all shining
For the loved ones dead and gone
We sing the song within our hearts to carry on

We grew up at the bingo
and we grew up on the field
we ran up through the woods
and wore their silence as a shield

we played that we were gypsies
we were cowboys we were huns
and we never had to play at Indians

They play "Maple Sugar
And it carries me back home
Dancing in the kitchen
With my crazy Uncle John
And with those Northern Lights all shining
For the loved ones dead and gone
We sing the song within our hearts to carry on

We hid from tales of Medicine
gone twisted dark and mean
still we looked for hidden footprints
from the ones who live between
we smiled and kept the secrets
when we saw and heard the signs
of how that world lives on in mystery
a song between the lines

They play "Maple Sugar"
And it carries me back home
Dancing in the kitchen
With my crazy Uncle John
And with those Northern Lights all shining
For the loved ones dead and gone
We sing the song within our hearts to carry on.

CHICKADEE: EGG, INTO THE FUTURE

waawan —	egg
waawiyeminagad —	it is globular
waazakone —	it glows

When I was a small girl, I began to see
the dream of my life before me; in our family
such a thing is not unusual.

wanisin —	it is lost; it gets lost
ningwaanakwad —	it is cloudy
noodin —	it is windy
webaasin —	it is blown away by the wind
weniban —	disappeared!; gone!

Curl your heart into the big, wild beat and feel
power of the drum, unfurl the power of surrender
is the naming

ozhibii'igan(an) —	something written, document
wa'aw —	this (animate)
wa'awedi —	this (animate)
waaban —	dawn

People die at dawn, but people begin then, too

waabang —	tomorrow
waasamowin —	electricity, lightning
wese'an —	it is a tornado

Breathe, egg. Breathe, bird.

noogibide —	it stops moving; it stops speeding

nookaa —	it is soft; it is tender
noominigan —	ointment, salve
ode'imin —	strawberry
ginibag —	rose flower

You aren't the only one at work building this world
curl into it, tiny

ombaasin —	it is lifted up by the wind
ombiwidoo -	lifts and carries it
onizhishin —	it is nice; it is good
oshki-ayi'ii(an) —	something new; something young

it glows, soft
new, this animate tomorrow

waaban

waabang

waawan

curl into the world.

FORMULAE FOR MOON AND TIME

POVERTY OF HISTORY

I wanted to write a poem
that would tell you, in the oldest tongues of our land
just how old and well beloved is this land, and by whom.

You must remain heedless, I have not the means
we are joined by a poverty of history, friend. It was taken
from me, I cannot pass on to you how to name
the pathways, lifeblood, river and mountain
planes of the face, of this land.

This beloved, we must address
with an amnesiac's desperation.

We have forgotten, by will or by violence, this
beloved's names. We call new names
and hope we are forgiven.

Uncharted seas may rise, or the land
may turn to us, like a wife
leans her cheek into to the cupped hand
of a forgetful, loving husband.

The truth is, I lie, friend. I've heard
of a time we lived like swallows
in a riverbank, in the sun; but if you
don't know the one, I can't tell you
more, nor smooth this cheek
with poetry. I tie my tongue and wear
my pockets inside out.

Poverty first, then history.

COFFEE AND TEA

There are things
we can reconcile
things we need not
my mother drank coffee

my father was for tea
he had an old brown betty
and when that broke
a tall aluminum pot
with a waist

a two or a three bag tea
sit a while or ponder longer
these are the things

in my work life
so much of my father
in my kitchen
coffee.

BEHIND THE MUSIC

The whole wide universe is singing, mystics say
So there's no way to ever go behind the music.

She liked the crashing of the cymbals, golden splay
Of splintered sound waves to and fro behind the music.

So many cautionary tales, or maybe just the one exists
Of how your red shoes dare not slow behind the music.

It's just a molecule of consequence, that little thing that twists
Between the minds of those who know, behind the music.

Every player come in thrall to ageless muse is forced to play
The whip keeps stinging, ancient, slow, behind the music.

Every mystic and musician rides the wake with shackled wrists
surfing the great song's undertow, behind the music.

BREATH OF LIFE

Perhaps I have sipped light from someone else's song
life given breath giving life that kindles light.

Shores of Lake Chapala, last faint hint of smoke
corn-stubble fires, whispering orchard, nightbird
call. Suddenly, stars.

Up North, checking the mares, their frosted brows
bare feet, rime-white straw, calm brown eyes
deep as sky. And then, night's dancers flare
eagle wing shawl above us all.

Streets of Seoul, Sewell seule, up early for downtime
from delegated work. Corner news stand sells seaweed
breakfast rolls. Ajima smile from owner. Secret
rainbows cast by sidewalk washers' plastic hoses
how nimble is the waking urban sun.

Perhaps the moon does not reflect voiced joys, but
refracts them, into a radiant plenty without regard for distance.

Does this little breath reach even into
plastic-littered depths where a child is
growing; war behind, in front, indifference
walls, guns, fences? Hungry ocean, tiny craft.

Perhaps this prayer may reach that round
pearled sounding board of the moon, or her
boomerang curl, sending only one breath, but enough
to the heart of a poet who needs to survive.

Perhaps it is for this that we are given the moon.

MAWI'OMI: UNVEILING

For the Mawi'omi at Acadia in September of 2015,
who brought me home

This was the fire in the night

this was the centre of the heart alight
deepest dreaming blinking in new sun
this was where we dared

to breathe together, entrained to
listening, first, skin tight with longing for
the drum to come that never left us
drum that drives this land we are this
land, if we are beautiful we are home.

Where the red dresses bleed, heal it with
sorrowful love, where the leaping
warriors lead, heal it with tumbling love
where the knowledge keepers stay
through night and through day, come
into the fire circle with it
listen, cry, dance, laugh, wonder
speak your dream, look up
you are already whole, already
home, where we dare our deepest
dream unfurling, shimmering in new
sun. Centre of the heart

alight, this is the fire in the night
called home. Mawi'omi.

SUMMER'S COWS

> *There is hope. There is hope everywhere.*
> *Today God gives milk, and I have the pail.*
> — "Snow" by Anne Sexton

Life is good. God is not my milk cow, but still
life is good, and I have known
some godly milk cows, aspects of divinity
glinting from hoof and horn and eye
humour in their well-aimed tails
flanks swelled   like Buddha's
belly against my cheek. Thus I have
no need to seek the Buddha in meditation
I have leaned against warm rumbling
goddess bellies, finding the rhythm
in hands, breath, voice
to match their heaven-scented air

the sure, epochal grind of bottom teeth
cows need own no upper incisors

how the goddesses sway across the fields
clover in their lips
hips cloaked in daring flies
(not a snowflake among them)
tails to clear the air.

No, God is not my milk cow
but my milk cow is divine
and life is good.

And have you seen the cows
at coffee klatsch?

out on the hillside maundering
along the ridgetop swell in flirtatious sun

while one among their number takers her turn
to gather close the sistren's calves
and lie in stately grandeur, in their midst.

Perhaps she teaches chewing the cud, perhaps
shares old tales of long gone times, auroch times

See, even now, two bull calves rise and caper off
with swaggering brows, to strut and butt and make
believe that they are hairy, fierce and wild.

The old one burps and blinks, content
they will soon enough come kneeling back
small square muzzles asking
where their mother's udder might be

and the sistren, as if on command
will come undulating down the rise
each with eyes only for her own.

And evening will settle, unbleached
flies buzzing counterpoint to tear, chew
rumble, belch, green organic paean of these
queens of ruminant goddesshood
and life is good.

HAIKU SUITE: URBAN GARDEN

Urban shepherdess
coax your electric goat through
the yard's pasturage.

Urban peasant queen
line your shelves with jewelry
raspberries in jars.

Urban daredevil
bushwhack through those pumpkin vines
bring the season down to earth.

Harvest this: there is
no sacred space made for prayers
save every place.

NOCTURNE: TINY NOW
For my beloved mom,
on the eve of her departure into the larger dance

She is tiny now, my mother
and jokes in the morning, when
her teeth aren't in, how she whistles
like a little bird. And i want to reach

back to the nights when
she brought the piglets in
laid them in the wood stove oven
so tiny, but she believed in them
and in that warm cradle, the spark
of life rekindled in them. How

do I cradle her? now
she is so tiny, softly
drawing nearer to
the Western Door.

This poem won't do it.

This poem is for me
a piglet grown, with
my astonished snout
of discovery, how the power
that built a world for me still
reveals itself, blue
slight, soft, tiny.

IF

If by my words here
I make you less or more
or other than you are
forgive me, for we
are none of us possible
to sum in words.

five is the number of fingers in a fist, or in a hand stretched open

inawemaagan(ag) —	relative(s)
weweni —	proper; correct
wii —	want to; will
wii —	want to; will
wiijiiwaagan(ag) —	companion; partner
wiisagaa —	it is bitter
wiishkoban —	it is sweet
zanagad —	it is difficult
zesegide'e —	my heart beats violently
zesegan —	little hail, it is hailing
wewiib —	hurry!; quick!
zesegide'e —	my heart beats violently (or exultant?)
zesika —	suddenly; unexpectedly; all of a sudden
zhigwa —	now; at this time
ziigwan —	it is spring
gizhaanimad —	there is a warm wind
gwekaanimad —	the wind shifts; the wind changes
zhingwaakoons —	young pine
ziibaaska'igan —	jingle (on dress)
zhawendaagwad —	it is blessed; it is pitied
zoongan —	it is solid; it is strong

ikidowin —   word
imaa —   there
inashke —   look!

mamaawi inawemaaganaq, sing now
hands open, like birds
in every language, one and any breath
is enough to say Yes.

A SONG FOR

after the holocaust
buffalo genocide
after the atom bomb
meltdown, the ddt
under the ozone hole
after the slick transfats begat the cancer
stats, after transit of mercury vaccines
water tables, marrow-bones, fish

red menace, yellow peril, black lives
matter after you know your place
idle no more after train blockades
lac megantic, after tidal waves
after the climate warms
greenland reclaims its name

after drowning cities beget
water wars, after the soda babies
starvation at their side after the dirty
bombs, drones, martyrs' suicides

after party's over, after menopause
when future hope becomes the tally
of my days; after the next beginning
whenever that thunderclap, keep
back a song for that, for ever
after all, for after all of that
a song is all we are at last.

A NOTE ON THE USAGE OF "I" AND "YOUS"

In some poems, I've chosen to use 'i' to correct the bias of English, in which first person is held proper, while others are common. I used to do this a lot. I've settled down.

The writer, Vera Wabegiizhig, introduced me to the deliberate reclamation of 'yous,' not as a signifier of ignorance, that we don't know the proper English plural, but as a celebration of dialects of English grafted on to roots with other rules.

NOTES

Versions of numerous poems in this book first appeared on prairiepomes.com, including:
"Creation Song", "One Moon Many Faces", "Omiimiikaa", "Making Stew", "Washing the World", "Th e Drunken Bicycles", "Ashes in the Making", "Turtle Island Easter Prayer", "Summer's Cows", and "Nocturne: Tiny Now".

"Chickadee Suite" — this poem began as shards gleaned from http://weshki.atwebpages.com/oj_dict.html.
Gchi Miigwech to those who kept Anishinaabemowin alive, and those who, through sites like these, work to stitch together our devastated tongues.

In 2015, I self-published a limited edition chapbook, Suite: Sisters, where "Free", "Barra de Navidad", and "Poem of Silence" first appeared.

"Hunting Season" was first published in *Writing the City: Poets Laureate of Edmonton 2005 – 13* (Douglas Barbour, Editor, Edmonton Arts Council, 2011), as were "The Mortal Summer", "Edmonton in Winter: This Pehonân", and "Bush-whacking".

"Shape-shifting" — Mi'gmaq is Listuguj orthography, for a word also rendered Mi'kmak and Micmac. Our language is Lnuisi, and thus I am also Lnu, or more specifically, Lnuskw.

"Meltwater" was published in Stroll of Poets Anthology 2013.

"Down by the Mary Burlie" — Mary Burlie was an Edmonton social worker and anti-poverty activist. After her death in 1996, the city named a tiny inner-city park for her. They also chose that park to host a bronze memorializing the Montreal Massacre.

"Moon Luna Personal" — *Gracias a* Leo Campos Aldunez for proofing my Spanish, and Giselle Lemire, *merci pour le même en Français*. Any quirks or outright fox poos are my own.

"Waiting for Genghis Khan" — Th e Beast is the wildfire that devastated Fort MacMurray, Alberta, in 2016; people fled down Highway 63, aka Th e Highway of Death. Most came back.

An early version of "Dark Season Prayer" was first published in a chapbook, *Dark Season*, for The Olive Reading Series, in 2012, along with "Atomic World", "She Sang", "things you give up", "Say That He Shall Be Given . . . ", and what became "Lonely Planet" and "Paths and Hills".

"Go Home Moon" — Mr. Yegpie tweets via @yegmagpie to all his friends in Edmonton, who don't question his remarkable typing skills. He graciously allowed me to quote this tweet. I leave cat food on the verandah. Pay artists.

"Mittens" was first published in Creative Connections, a yearlong, multidisciplinary, intergenerational exchange between The Learning Centre Literacy Association and Edmonton Christian Northeast School, sponsored by the Edmonton Arts Council. Pat Cole, then eighty-seven, wrote, painted, sculpted, and knit mittens to share among us.

"Knit" was commissioned for the Day of Awareness of Violence Against Seniors, in 2013. I didn't know, I said, how to write about Elder Abuse; Betty knew better. An early version of this poem was published for the members of Seniors' Association of Greater Edmonton.

"Edmonton In Winter: This Pehonân" — Pehonân, as i understand it, is a Cree word meaning 'gathering place.' Where

Edmonton sits, there has been a Pehonân, seasonally occupied, for something like 8000 years.

"Barra de Navidád" — "Megwetch" — this is how my sisters and I first saw "miigwech" written, how we first wrote it. Orthographies change, meaning remains. It's Anishinaabemowin for "thank you".

Mawi'omi is a Mi'gmaq word that, as I understand it, is both noun and verb, signifying Gathering, Sacred Fire and also Administrative District. There are seven Mawi'omi in Mi'kmak'i. My family connection is to Listuguj, in the Gespe'gewa'gi Mawiomi. Acadia belongs to the Sipekni'katik (Sugapune'gati /Shubenacadie) Mawi'omi.

ACKNOWLEDGMENTS

Thanks to Trish Sewell for cover art, beta reading, inspiration and unflagging belief.

Thanks also to Shelley A. Leedahl, Randy Kohan, Richard Lemm & Lee Ellen Pottie, UPEI, Andrea Schenke Wyile, Elders Joe Michael & the late Doug Knockwood, Acadia University, St Francis Xavier University, Lennox Island First Nation School, Stephen Humphrey, Kris Demeanor, Janet Marie Rogers, Rayanne Haines & Edmonton Poetry Festival, Stroll of Poets, Edmonton Arts Council, Leo, Giselle, Thistledown Press, and my families great and small.

ANNA MARIE SEWELL'S poetry is part of the Ukrainian Shumka Dancers production *Ancestors & Elders* (world premiere April 27). Her debut collection, *Fifth World Drum* (Frontenac Press, 2009) will be joined in September by *For the Changing Moon* (Thistledown Press). Anna Marie was Edmonton's 4th Poet Laureate (2011 to 2013), and created *The Poem Catcher* public art installation at Edmonton's City Hall. A multi-disciplinary artist, Anna Marie's practice centres on collaborative projects, and her writing plays across boundaries of language, culture, and worldview. *www. prairiepomes.com.*